Anton
BRUCKNER

Mass in E minor
WAB 27
(1882 version)

(Kurt Soldan)

Vocal Score
Klavierauszug

SERENISSIMA MUSIC, INC.

CONTENTS

ORCHESTRA

2 Oboes, 2 Clarinets, 2 Bassoons
4 Horns, 2 Trumpets, 3 Trombones
Timpani,

Duration: ca. 40 minutes
First performance:
September 29, 1869
Linz, Cathedral of the Immaculate Conception
Soli, Chorus and Ensemble conducted by the composer
Revised Version
Linz, Cathedral of the Immaculate Conception, 1885
Soli, Chorus and Ensemble
Adalbert Schreyer, conductor

Complete orchestral parts compatible with this vocal score are available (Cat. No. A2582) from
E. F. Kalmus & Co., Inc.
6403 West Rogers Circle
Boca Raton, FL 33487 USA
(800) 434 - 6340
www.kalmus-music.com

Mass in E minor
WAB 27
(1882 version)

1. Kyrie

Anton Bruckner (1824-1896)
Piano reduction by Kurt Soldan

SERENISSIMA MUSIC, INC.

21
A
Sopr
- i - son.
- i - son.
Alt
- i - son.
- i - son.
Ten
p cresc.
Ky-ri-e e-le-i-son, Ky-ri-e e-le-i-
p cresc.
Ky- -ri-e e-le-i-son, Ky-ri-e e-le-i-
Baß
p cresc
Ky - ri-e e-le-i-son, Ky-ri-e e-le-i-
p cresc.
Ky - ri - e e - le-i-son, Ky-ri-e e-le-i-
f
32
B
mf
Chri - - -
mf
Chri - - -
ff dim.
-son, Ky-ri-e e-le- - - - - - - - i-son.
-son, Ky-ri-e e-le- - - - - - - - i-son.
-son, Ky-ri-e e-le- - - - - - - - i-son.
-son, Ky-ri-e e-le- - - - - - son.
ff

41
Sopr.
Chri - ste e - le-i-son, Chri - ste, Chri-ste, Chri - -
-ste, Chri-ste e-le-i-son, e - le-i-son, Chri - - ste, Chri - -
Alt
- - ste, Chri - - - ste, Chri - ste e - le - i - son,
Chri - - ste, Chri - - - ste e -
Ten
Baß
Chri - - ste
Chri-
41
50
Sopr
- - ste, Chri - - - ste
-ste, Chri - - ste e - le - i -
Alt
Chri - - ste, Chri - - ste, Chri-
-le - i - son, Chri - - - -
Ten
Chri - - ste, Chri - - - -
Chri - - ste e - le - i - son,
Baß
e - le - i - son, e - le - i - son, e-
- - ste, Chri - ste, Chri - ste e - le - i - son,
50

4

78
Sopr
-le - i - son, Ky - ri - e e - le - - i - son,
-le - i - son, Ky - ri - e e - lei - son, e - le - i - son, Ky -
Alt
-le - i - son, Ky - ri - e e - le - i - son,
-le - i - son, Ky - ri - e e - le - i - son, e - le - i - son,
Ten
Ky - ri - e, Ky - ri - e, Ky -
Ky - ri - e, Ky - ri - e e - le - i - son,
Baß
Ky - ri -
Ky - ri - e, Ky -
f
mf
p
dim.
87
E
Sopr
Ky - ri - e, Ky - ri - e,
- ri - e, Ky - ri - e e - le - i - son, Ky - ri - e, Ky - ri - e,
Alt
Ky - ri - e, Ky - ri - e, Ky - ri - e,
Ky - ri - e, Ky - ri - e, Ky - ri - e,
Ten
- ri - e, Ky - ri - e, Ky - ri - e, Ky - ri - e,
Ky - ri - e, Ky - ri - e, Ky - ri - e,
Baß
- e, Ky - ri - e e - le - i - son, Ky - ri - e, Ky - ri - e,
- ri - e e - le - i - son, Ky - ri - e, Ky - ri - e,
ff

F
96
Sopr
Alt
Ten.
Baß
dim.
p
pp
Ky - - - ri - e e - le - i - son, Ky - ri - e e - le - i - son, Ky - - - -
Ky - - - ri - e e - le - i - son, Ky - ri - e e - le - i - son, Ky - - - -
Ky - - - ri - e, Ky - ri - e e - le - i - son, e - le - i - son, e - lei - son,
Ky - - - ri - e, Ky - ri - e e - le - i - son, e - le - i - son, e - lei - son
Ky - - - ri - e, Ky - ri - e e - le - i - son, e - le - i - son, Ky - ri - e,
Ky - - - ri - e, Ky - ri - e e - le - i - son, e - le - i - son, Ky - ri - e,
Ky - - - ri - e, Ky - ri - e e - le - - i - son, e - lei - son,
Ky - - - ri - e, Ky - ri - e e - le - - i - son, e - lei - son,
107
- - - - - - - - ri - e, Ky - ri - e e - le - i - son.
- - - - - - - - ri - e, Ky - ri - e e - le - i - son.
e - lei - son, e - lei - son, Ky - ri - e e - le - i - son.
e - lei - son, e - lei - son, Ky - ri - e e - le - i - son.
Ky - ri - e, Ky - ri - e, Ky - ri - e e - le - i - son.
Ky - ri - e, Ky - ri - e, Ky - ri - e e - le - i - son
e - lei - son, e - lei - son, Ky - ri - e e - le - i - son.
e - lei - son, e - lei - son, Ky - ri - e e - le - i - son.

2. Gloria

Sopran

Et in ter - ra pax ho - mi - ni - bus bo - næ vo - lun - ta - tis. Lau-

Alt

Et in ter - ra pax ho - mi - ni - bus bo - næ vo - lun - ta - tis. Lau-

Tenor

Lau-

Baß

Lau-

-da - mus te, be - ne - di - ci - mus te, ad - o - ra - - mus te, glo - ri - fi-

-da - mus te, be - ne - di - ci - mus te, ad - o - ra - - mus te,

-da - mus te, be - ne - di - ci - mus te, ad - o - ra - - mus te, glo - ri - fi-

-da - mus te, be - ne - di - ci - mus te, ad - o - ra - - mus te, glo - ri - fi-

-ca - - mus, glo - ri - fi - ca - mus te. Gra - ti - as

glo - ri - fi - ca - mus, glo - ri - fi - ca - mus te.

-ca - - mus, glo - ri - fi - ca - mus te.

glo - ri - fi - ca - mus, glo - ri - fi - ca - mus te.

22
B
a - gi-mus ti - - bi propter magnam glo-ri-am tu - am.
Gra - ti - as propter ma-gnam glo-ri-am tu - am.
Gra - ti - as propter ma-gnam glo-ri-am tu - am. Do -
Gra - ti - as propter ma-gnam glo-ri-am tu - am.
dim.
30
Do - mi - ne_ De - us, Rex cœ-le-stis, De-us Pa - ter
Do - mi - ne_ De - us,_ Rex cœ-le-stis, De-us Pa - ter
- mi-ne De - - us, Rex cœ-le-stis, De-us Pa-ter, De-us Pa - ter
De-us Pa - ter
38
C
o - mni-po-tens. Do - mi - ne_ Fi -
o - mni-po-tens. Do - mi - ne_
o - mni-po-tens. Do - mi-ne Fi - li
o - mni-po-tens. Do - mi-ne Fi -
dim.

45
ff
-li u - ni - ge-ni-te Je - - su Chri -
ff
Fi - - li u - ni - ge-ni-te Je - - su, Je - su Chri -
ff
u-ni - ge - ni-te Je - - su, Je - - - su Chri -
ff
- - li u-ni - ge - ni-te Je - - su, Je - su Chri -
cresc
ff
52
-ste. Do - mi-ne De-us, A - gnus De - i, Fi - li-us Pa -
-ste. Do - mi-ne De-us, A - gnus De - i, Fi - li-us Pa -
-ste. Do - mi-ne De-us, A - gnus De - i, Fi - li-us Pa -
-ste. Do - mi-ne De-us, A - gnus De - i, Fi - li-us Pa -
59
rit.
-tris
-tris
-tris.
-tris.
p dolce
pp

D
Andante
Qui tol - lis pec-ca-ta mun - di,
Qui tol - lis pec-ca-ta mun - di,
Mi - se - re - re no - bis.
Mi - se - re - re no - bis.
p dolce
Qui tol - lis pec-ca-ta mun - di,
Qui tol - lis pec-ca-ta mun - di,
E
sus - ci-pe
sus - ci-pe
sus - ci-pe
sus - ci-pe
p dolce
de - pre - ca - ti - o - nem no-stram. Qui se - des ad dex - te-ram
de - pre - ca - ti - o - nem no-stram. Qui se - des ad dex - te-ram
de - pre - ca - ti - o - nem no-stram. Qui se - des ad dex - te-ram
de - pre - ca - ti - o - nem no-stram. Qui se - des ad dex - te-ram
cresc.

F
ritard.
Pa-tris, mi - se - re - re, mi - se - re - re, mi - se - re - re no - bis.
Pa-tris, mi - se - re - re, mi - se - re - re, mi - se - re - re no - bis.
Pa-tris, mi-se - re-re no - bis.
mi-se - re-re no - bis.
poco a poco accel.
G Tempo I
Quo - ni - am tu so-lus san - ctus, tu so-lus Do - mi - nus. Tu
Quo - ni - am tu so-lus san - ctus, tu so-lus Do - mi - nus.
Quo - ni-am tu so-lus san - ctus, tu so-lus Do-mi - nus, tu so - lus al - tis - si - mus,
tu so-lus Do-mi - nus, tu solus al - tis-si - mus,

so - lus al - tis - si - mus, Je - su Chri - ste.

tu so-lus al - tis - si - mus, Je - su Chri - ste.

Je - su Chri - ste.

Je - su Chri - ste.

Cum San - cto Spi - ri - tu, in glo - ri - a De -

Cum San - cto Spi - ri - tu, in glo - ri - a De -

Cum San - cto Spi - ri - tu, in glo - ri - a De -

Cum San - cto Spi - ri - tu, in glo - ri - a De -

Pa - - - - - - - - - - tris.

Pa - - - - - - - - - - tris.

Pa - - - - - - - - - - tris.

Pa - - - - - - - - - - tris.

131
I
A - men, a - - - men,
A - - men, a - men, a -
A - men, a - - - men, a - - - men,
A - - men, a - men, a -
131
I
139
K
a - - men, a - men, a - men, a - - - - - men, a - men,
- men, a - - - men, a - - men, a - - - men, a - men, a -
a - - men, a - men, a - men, a - men, a - - - - - - - men,
- men, a - men, a - - - men, a - men, a - men,
139
K
147
a - - - - men, a - men, a - men, a - - - men, a -
- men, a - - - men, a - men, a - men, a - men, a - - - - - -
a - men, a - men, a - men, a - - - men,
a - - - men, a - men, a - men, a - men, a - - - - - - -
147

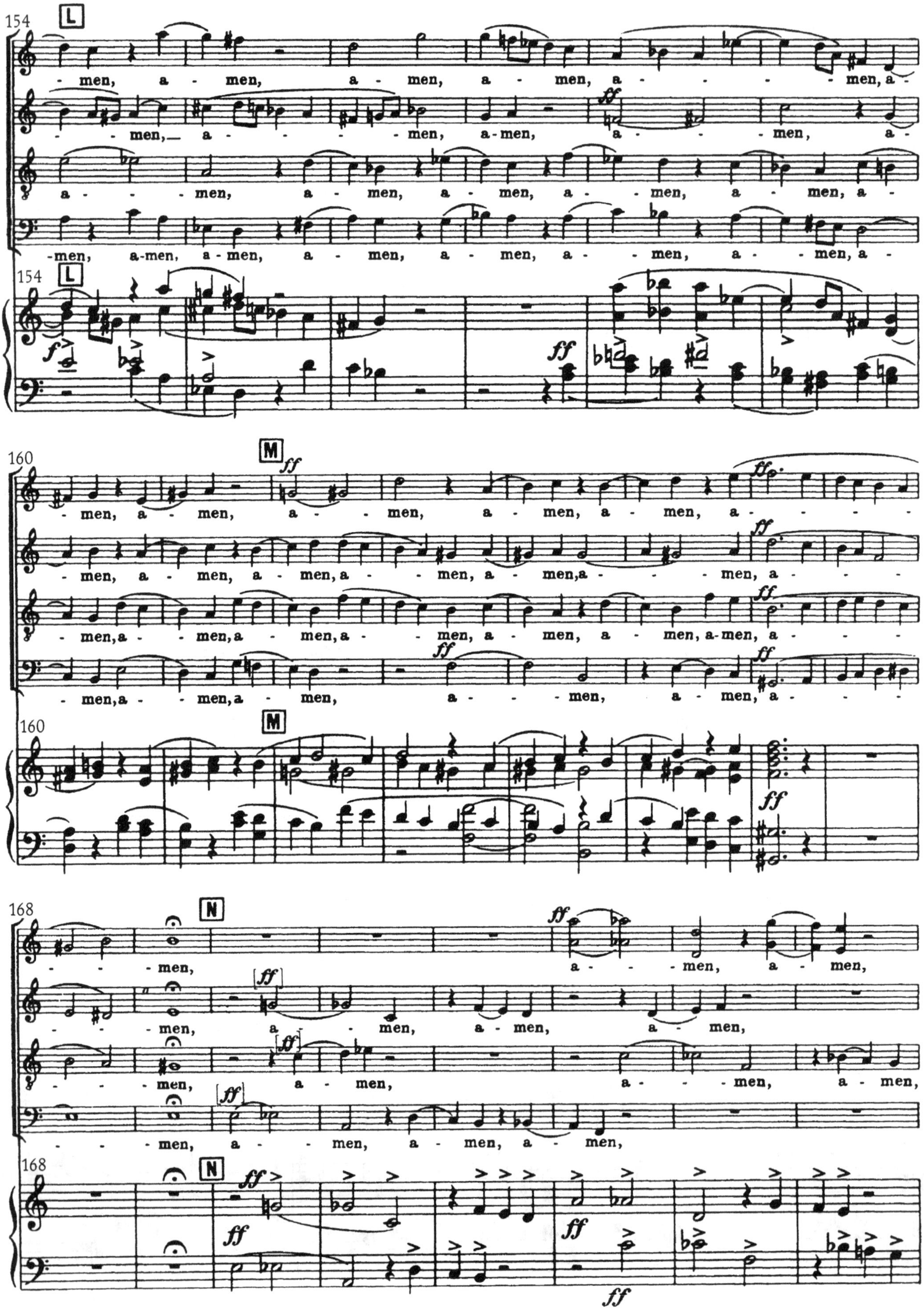

176
O
ff
a - - - - - men, a - - - - - men,
a - - - - - men, a - - - - - men,
a - - - - - men, a - - - - - men,
a - - - - - men, a - - - - - men,
sempre ff
180
a - - - - - - - - men, a - - - men, a -
a - - - - - - - - men, a - - - men, a -
a - - - - - - - - men, a - - - men, a -
a - - - - - - - - men, a - - - men, a -
186
-men, a - men, a - men, a - men, a - - - - men.
-men, a - men, a - men, a - men, a - - - - men.
-men, a - men, a - men, a - men, a - - - - men.
-men, a - men, a - men, a - men, a - - - - men.

3. Credo

B
o - mni-a — sæ-cu-la.
De-um de — De-o, lu-men de —
lu-mi-ne, De - um ve-rum de De-o ve - ro,
ge-ni-tum, non fa-ctum,
consub-stanti-a-lem Pa-tri,
per — quem o - mni-a fa - cta
8va

C
mf
sunt. qui pro - pter nos ho - mines, et propter no - stram sa -
lu - tem de - scen - dit de coe - - - lis.
f
ff
dim.
ritard.
D
Adagio
p
pp
Et in - car - na - tus est de
Et incar-na-tus est de
Et incar-na-tus est

56
dim.
pp
p
Spi-ri-tu Sancto ex Ma-ri - a Vir - gi-ne, et ho-mo factus est,
Spi-ri-tu Sancto ex Ma-ri - a Vir - gi-ne, et ho-mo factus est,
de Spi-ri-tu Sancto ex Ma-ri-a Vir - gi-ne, et ho-mo factus est,
et ho-mo factus est,
de Spi-ri-tu Sancto ex Ma-ri-a Vir - gi-ne,
63
et — in-car-na - tus est de Spi-ri-tu Sancto ex — Ma-ri - a Vir - gi-ne, et
Spi-ri-tu Sancto ex Ma-ri - a Vir - gi-ne, et
et — incarna-tus est de
Vir - gi - ne,
et — incarna-tus est de Spi-ri-tu Sancto ex Ma-ri-a Vir - gi-ne, et
de Spi-ri-tu Sancto ex Ma-ri-a Vir - gi-ne,
68
E
ho-mo factus est Cru - ci - fi -
ho-mo factus est. Cru - ci - fi -
ho-mo factus est. Cru - ci - fi -
et ho-mo factus est. Cru - ci - fi -
legato

74
cresc.
dim.
xus, cru - - - - ci - fi - - xus
xus, cru - - - - ci - fi - - xus
xus, cru - - - - ci - fi - - xus
xus, cru - - - - ci - fi - - xus
79
F
p
pp
e - ti-am pro no - bis. sub Pon - ti-o Pi-la - to pas - sus,
e - ti-am pro no - bis. sub Pon - ti-o Pi-la - to pas - sus,
e - ti-am pro no - bis. sub Pon - ti - o Pi - la - to pas - sus,
e - ti-am pro no - bis. sub Pon - ti - o Pi - la - to pas - sus,
84
ppp
pas - sus, et se - pul - tus est.
pas - sus, et se - pul - tus est.
pas - sus, et se - pul - tus est.
pas - sus, et se - pul - tus est.

93
G Allegro
sempre ff
Et re - sur - re -
f sempre cresc
Et re - sur - re - xit ter - ti - a
pp cresc.
ff
98
xit ter - ti - a di - e, se - cun - dum scri -
di - e, se - cun - dum scri -
102
sempre ff
ptu - ras, se - cun - dum scri - ptu - ras.

107
H
et a - scendit in coelum: se - det ad dex - teram,
et a - scendit in coelum: se - det ad dex - teram,
et a - scendit in coelum: se - det ad dex - teram, se - det ad
et a - scendit in coelum: se - det ad dex - teram, se - det ad
112
se - det ad dex - te-ram Pa - - tris,
se - det ad dex - te-ram Pa - - tris,
dex - - te-ram Pa - - tris,
dex - - te-ram Pa - - tris,
116
I
sempre ff
et i - te-rum ven - tu -
et i - te-rum ven - tu -
et i - terum ven - tu -
et i - terum ven - tu -

120
fff
rus est cum glo - ri -
124
a, cum glo - ri - a
K
poco a poco cresc.
p poco a poco cresc.
ju-di-ca - re, ju-di-ca - re, ju-di-
ju-di-ca-re, ju-di-ca-re,
ju - di - ca - re,
dim
p
poco a poco cresc
mf

24

Z258291

155
M Tempo I
Et in Spi-ri-tum san-ctum, Do-mi-num, et vi-vi-fi - can-tem: qui ex Pa - tre Fi-li - o-que pro-ce -
dit. Qui cum Pa-tre, et Fi - li - o si-mul ad - o - ra -
162
N
dim.
170
tur, et con - glo - ri - fi - ca - tur: qui lo - cu-tus est per pro-phe -

178
O
ff ben marcato
tas. Et u - nam san - ctam ca - tho - li - cam et
p
ff
183
ff sempre
a - po - sto - li - cam ec - cle - si - am. Con -
a - po - sto - li - cam ec - cle - si - am Con - fi - te - or
188
fi - te - or u - num ba - pti - sma in re -
u - num ba - pti - sma in re -

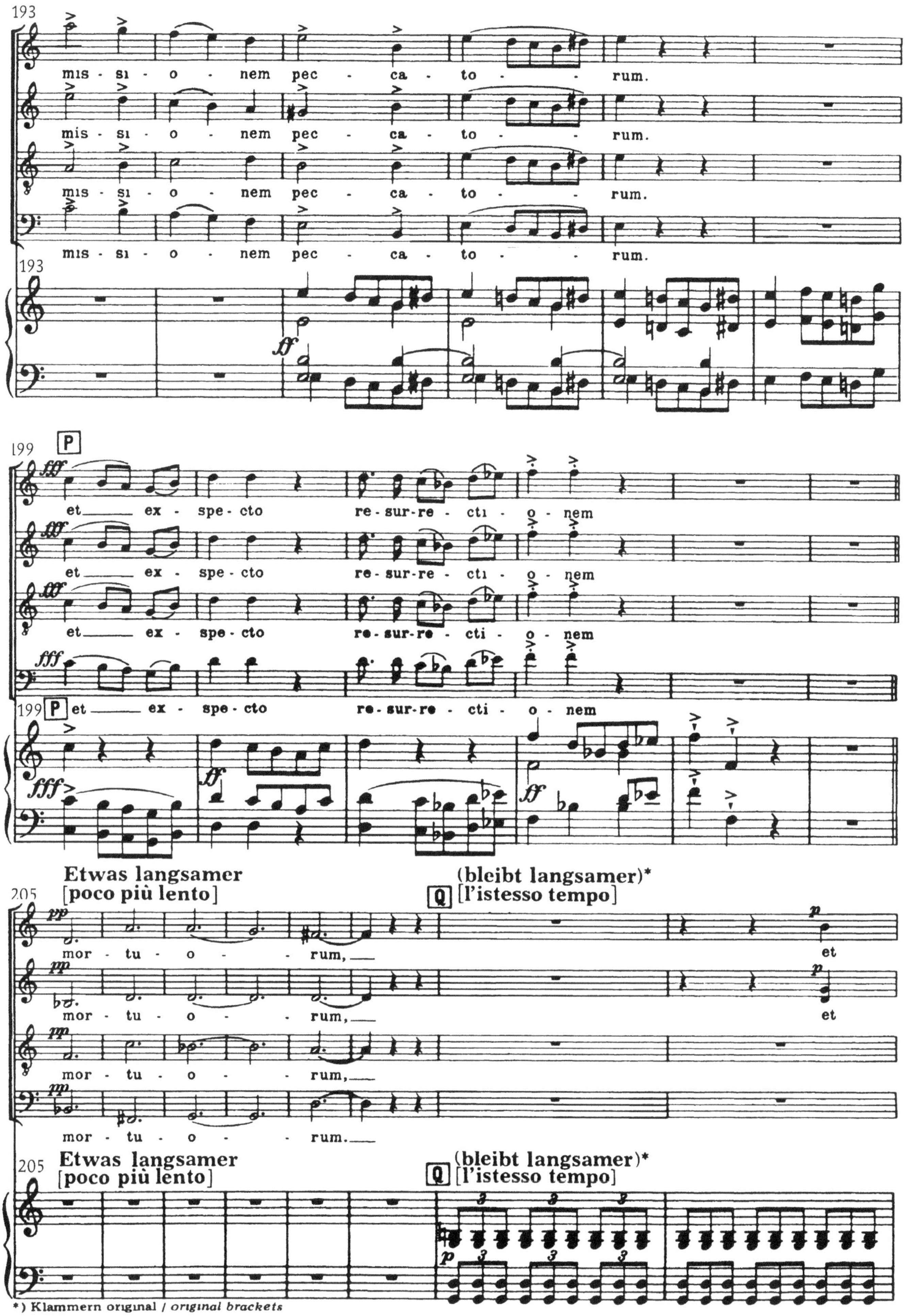

*) Klammern original / *original brackets*

213
mf cresc.
vi - tam ven - tu - ri sæ - cu - li. A - men,
mf cresc.
vi - tam ven - tu - ri sæ - cu - li. A - men,
p cresc. mf f cresc
et vi - tam ven - tu - ri sæ - cu - li.
p cresc. mf f cresc.
et vi - tam ven - tu - ri sæ - cu - li.
213
cresc.
217
fff sempre
a - - - men,
fff sempre
a - - - men,
fff sempre
a - - - men,
fff sempre
a - - - men,
217
fff sempre
221
a - - - men.
a - - - men.
a - - - men.
a - - - men.
221

4. Sanctus

14
Sopr.
Alt
Ten.
Baß
ctus, san - - - - ctus, san
san - - - - - - - - - - - - - ctus,
ctus, san - - ctus, san - - - - - ctus, san-ctus,
ctus, san - - - - - - - ctus, san - - - - - ctus,
ctus, san - - - - - ctus, san - ctus, san
san - - - ctus, san - - - ctus,
ctus, san-ctus, san - - - - - - - - - - ctus, san
ctus, san - - - - - - ctus, san - - - ctus, san
14
20
ctus, san-ctus, san - ctus, san-ctus, san
san - - - ctus, san - - - - - - ctus, san
san - - - - - ctus, san - - - - - - - ctus, san
san - ctus, san - - - - - ctus, san
ctus, san
san - - - - - ctus, san - - - - - - - ctus, san
ctus, san - ctus, san - ctus, san - - ctus, san
ctus, san - - ctus, san - - - ctus, san
20

26
B
Sopr
Alt
Ten
Baß
ctus Do - - mi-nus De - us Sa - ba - oth.
fff
p cresc.
32
C
Ple - ni sunt coe - li et ter - ra glo - - ri - a

38
D
Sopr
Alt
Ten
Baß
tu - - - - a.
fff
ho - san - na
ff
sempre fff
44
in ex - cel - - - - - - - - - sis.
f

5. Benedictus

14
A
no-mi-ne Do-mi - ni, qui ve - nit in no-mi-ne Do-mi - ni, be - ne-
no-mi-ne Do-mi - ni, qui ve - nit in no-mi-ne Do-mi - ni, be - ne-
no-mi ne Do-mi - ni, qui ve - nit in no-mi-ne Do-mi - ni, be - ne-
poco a poco cresc
qui ve-nit in no - - mi-ne Do-mi - ni,
poco a poco cresc
qui ve-nit in no - - mi-ne Do-mi - ni,
21
B
cresc
di-ctus, be - ne - di-ctus, be - - ne - di - ctus qui
di-ctus, be - ne - di-ctus, be - - - ne - di - ctus qui
di-ctus, be - ne - di-ctus, be - - ne - di - ctus qui
p cresc
be - - ne - di - - ctus,
be - - ne - di - - ctus,

27
ve - - nit in no - mi - ne Do - mi - ni,
ve - - nit in no - mi - ne Do - mi - ni,
ve - - nit in no - mi - ne Do - mi - ni,
f
be - - - - - ne - di - - - ctus, be - ne -
f
be - - - ne - - - - - di - - - ctus, be - ne-
27
f
30
p
be - ne - di - - ctus_ qui_
p
be - ne di - - - ctus qui ve - - nit, qui
p
be - ne di - - - ctus qui ve - - - - - - - -
di - - - ctus_ qui_ ve - nit,
p
di - ctus, be - ne - di - ctus, be - - ne - - -
30
p

33
C
dim.
ve - nit, qui ve - nit,
ve - nit in no - - - mi - ne Do - - - -
- nit in no - - - mi - ne Do - - -
p
(dim.)
qui ve - nit, qui
di - ctus, be - ne - di - ctus, be - ne -
33
C
36
cresc.
pp
be - ne - di - ctus, qui ve - nit, qui
cresc
- mi - ni, be - ne - di - ctus, qui ve - nit, qui
cresc.
- mi - ni, be - ne - di - ctus, qui ve - nit,
cresc
ve - nit, be - ne - di - ctus, qui ve - nit, qui
cresc
di - ctus, be - ne - di - ctus, qui ve - nit, qui
36
cresc.
pp

39
D
f
dim.
p
ve - nit in no - mi - ne Do - mi - ni,
ve - nit in no - mi - ne Do - mi - ni,
pp
cresc
be - - ne - di - ctus, be - ne - di - ctus,
ve - nit in no - mi - ne Do - mi - ni,
ve - nit in no - mi - ne Do - mi - ni,
pp
43
be - ne - di - ctus,
be - ne - di - ctus,
qui ve - nit, qui ve - - - -
be - ne - di - ctus,
be - ne - di - ctus,

46
sempre cresc.
qui ve - nit, be - - ne -
sempre cresc.
qui ve - nit, be - - ne - -
sempre cresc.
- - - - nit, be - - ne -
sempre cresc.
qui ve - nit, be - ne - -
qui ve - nit,
46
sempre cresc.
49
di - ctus, be - - ne - di - ctus,
di - ctus, be - - ne - - di - ctus,
di - ctus, be - - ne - di - ctus,
di - - ctus, be - - ne - - di - - ctus,
sempre cresc
qui ve - - nit, be - ne -
49

52
E
dim. sempre
be - - ne - di - ctus, be - ne -
dim. sempre
be - - ne - - di - ctus, be - ne -
dim. sempre
be - - ne - di - ctus, be - ne -
dim. sempre
be - - ne - - di - ctus, be - ne -
dim. sempre
di - - ctus, be - ne - di - ctus qui
52
E
Kl.
dim. sempre
di - ctus qui ve - nit in no - mi - ne Do - mi - ni,
di - ctus qui ve - nit in no - mi - ne Do - mi - ni,
di - ctus qui ve - nit in no - mi - ne Do - mi - ni,
di - ctus qui ve - nit in no - mi - ne Do - mi - ni,
ve - nit in no - mi - ne, no - mi - ne Do - mi - ni,

60
F
be - ne - di - ctus qui ve - nit,
be - ne - di - ctus qui ve - nit,
be - ne - dı - ctus qui ve - nit, qui
be - ne - di - ctus, be - ne -
be - ne - di - ctus, be - ne -
legato sempre
65
cresc.
qui ve - nit in no - mi-ne Do - mi-ni,
qui ve - nit in no - mi-ne Do - mi-ni,
ve - nit in no - mı-ne Do - mi-ni,
di - ctus, be - ne - di - ctus qui
di - ctus, be - ne - di - ctus qui

70
p dim
pp
qui ve - nit in no-mi-ne Do-mi - ni,
qui ve - nit in no-mi-ne Do-mi - ni,
qui ve - nit in no-mi-ne Do-mi - ni,
dim
cresc.
ve - nit in no - mi-ne Do - mi - ni, in no - mi-ne Do - mi-
dim.
pp
poco a poco cresc.
75
G
f
qui ve - nit in no - mi-ne Do-mi - ni,
qui ve - nit in no - mi-ne Do-mi - ni,
qui ve - nit in no - mi-ne Do-mi - ni,
ni, qui ve - nit in no-mi-ne Do-mi - ni, be - ne -
ni, qui ve - nit in no-mi-ne Do-mi - ni, be - ne -
p
p dim
dim
Pos

80
qui — ve-nit, be - ne - di-ctus. Ho - san-na in ex-cel-sis, ho -
qui — ve-nit, be - ne - di-ctus. Ho - san-na in ex-cel-sis, ho -
qui — ve-nit, be - ne - di-ctus. Ho - san-na in ex-cel-sis, ho -
di-ctus, be - ne - di-ctus. Ho - san-na in ex-cel-sis, ho -
di-ctus, be - ne - di-ctus. Ho - san-na in ex-cel-sis, ho -
86
cresc
san - na in — ex - cel - - sis, ho - san - na in ex - cel - sis.
san - na in — ex - cel - - sis, ho - san - na in ex - cel - sis.
san - na in ex - cel - - sis, ho - san - na in ex - cel - sis.
san - na in ex - cel - - sis, ho - san - na in ex - cel - sis.
san - na in ex - cel - - sis, ho - san - na in ex - cel - sis.

6. Agnus Dei

12
Sopr
Alt
Ten
Baß
re - re, mi-se-re-re no - bis.
no - bis, mi-se-re-re no - bis
mi-se - re - re no - bis.
ff
pp
dim (pp)
p
Pos Trp
20
B
Sopr.
Alt
Ten.
Baß
p
poco a poco cresc.
A-gnus De - i, qui tol - lis pec-ca-ta mun - di:
poco a poco cresc
f

27
C
Sopr.
Alt
Ten.
Baß
p poco a poco cresc.
mf cresc.
f cresc
mi - se - re - re, mi - se -
mi - se - re - re, mi - se -
mi - se - re - re, mi - se - re - re,
mi - se - re - re, mi - se -
mi - se - re - re, mi - se - re - re, mi - se -
mi - se - re - re, mi - se - re -
mi - se - re - re no - bis, mi - se -
mi - se - re - re, mi - se -
32
ff
pp
-re - re, mi - se - re - re no - bis, mi - se -
-re - re, mi - se - re - re no - bis,
mi - se - re - re no - bis, mi - se -
-re - re, mi - se - re - re no - bis,
-re - re, mi - se - re - re no - bis, mi - se -
-re, mi - se - re - re no - bis,
-re - re, mi - se - re - re no - bis,
-re - re, mi - se - re - re no - bis, mi - se -

37
Sopr.
Alt
Ten.
Baß
cresc sempre
dim.
pp
re-re, mi-se-re-re, mi-se-re-re no-bis.
mi-se-re-re no-bis.
p
D
45
poco a poco cresc.
A-gnus De-i, qui tol-lis, qui tol-lis, qui tol-
A-gnus De-i, qui tol-lis, qui

50
E
Sopr
Alt
Ten.
Baß
pp
-lis, qui tol - lis pec-ca-ta mun - di: do - na no-bis pa -
tol - lis pec-ca-ta mun - di: do - na no-bis pa -
dim
55
F
pp sempre
p
mezza voce
mf
-cem, do - na no-bis pa - cem, do - na,

62
G
Sopr.
Alt
Ten.
Baß
dim
dim.
pp
mezza voce
falsetto
do - na pa - cem,
do - na,
Pos.
p
68
p cresc.
f dim sempre
f dim. sempre
pp
do - na no - bis pa - cem.
p cresc
Pos

www.ingramcontent.com/pod-product-compliance
Lightning Source LLC
Chambersburg PA
CBHW081600040426

42445CB00014B/1779